"Practice kind randomness and beautiful acts of senselessness."

– Anonymous MindF∗cker

Would you rather...?'s

MindF*cKs

Over 800 Ways to Confound, Confuse, and Abuse.

by Justin Heimberg & David Gomberg

Published by Seven Footer Press
247 West 30th Street, 11th Floor
New York, NY 10001

First Printing, June 2008
10 9 8 7 6 5 4
© Copyright Justin Heimberg and David Gomberg, 2008
All Rights Reserved

Would You Rather...?® is a registered trademark
used under license from Falls Media LLC, an Imagination company

Design by Tom Schirtz

ISBN-13 978-1-934734-01-8

www.sevenfooterpress.com

Why MindF*cks?

The situations and locations in this book are familiar to all of us. They're places or times where unspoken rules have sucked the life out of the proceedings, where people have become robots, and convention and seriousness have come to rule.

The mission of *MindF*cks* is to take on the institutions of seriousness, routine, and conformity; to arm you and fellow MindF*ckers with ways to wreak a little harmless havoc in everyday life.

But rest guiltlessly assured that your crimes serve a higher purpose. You are the Robin Hood of awkwardness. Your odd acts force the world to awaken from its slumber and experience the enlightened state of confusion/annoyance/transcendence that a good MindF*ck offers.

And it's also just kind of fun to screw with people.

TABLE OF CONTENTS

D&D

The word MindF∗ck, with or without the asterisk or capitalization, suggests different things to different people. The definition of MindF∗ck we are concerned with is the following:

MindF∗ck *n.* an act that confuses, discombobulates, or unsettles another person or persons without causing actual harm;
v. to intentionally perform such an act

To clarify, we do not mean "MindF∗ck" in the sense of manipulating someone for a power trip. Nor do we mean "MindF∗ck" literally, as in penetrating the brain with your phallus through ocular or nasal orifices. That's a different book. And God bless you if it's on your shelf. ☺

Disclaimer: The authors disclaim the shit out of any responsibility for any harm you may cause yourself and others. These lists are meant for entertainment purposes only. Of course, we aren't your parents and we can't tell you what to do, so if you are inspired to do something odd but amusing, that's your choice.

31 Things to **Do** at a **Job Interview** to **Screw** with the **Interviewer**

Few experiences are as humbling as a job interview. That big-shot behind the big desk has all the power and is sure to let you know it. No job is worth the ass-kissing and faux-chumminess a job interview requires. So why not turn the tables and make the interviewer far more uncomfortable than you are?

1. At the top of your resume, print (in italics) song lyrics that inspire you, such as:

   I would fight for you - I'd lie for you
   Walk the wire for you - yeah I'd die for you
   You know it's true.
   Everything I do - I do it for you.
   – Bryan Adams (from *Robin Hood, Prince of Thieves*)

2. Smell your fingers periodically.

3. Quote Jesus a little too often.

4. Need a ride home.

5. Refer to yourself several times as a "grown-ass man", as in "I don't need micromanaging. I'm a grown-ass man."

6 Bring an "attorney" to your interview. Consult the attorney whenever you're asked a question, and have the attorney whisper to you before answering.

7 Wink frequently.

8 Bring a pocket dictionary. Every time the interviewer mentions a mildly sophisticated word, open the dictionary, look up the word, repeat the definition quietly, and then close the dictionary and answer the question normally.

9 List all of your references as "Deceased".

10 Listen attentively to the interviewer's explanation of the company. Then, with a deadpan expression, point to the appropriate body parts and say "Milk, milk, lemonade, 'round the corner, fudge is made." (Perfect opportunity to wink.)

⑪ For the whole interview, stare an inch and a half above the interviewer's eyes.

⑫ Have a little bit of blood on your hands.

⑬ Take feverish notes. Constantly. Even when you are talking.

⑭ Suddenly jerk your head to one side and stare off for a few seconds. Repeat, if necessary.

⑮ As a follow-up to the interview, instead of sending thank you notes, send mix-tapes of songs that are somewhat uncomfortable (e.g., "Take on Me"; "I Want you to Want Me"; "Call Me".)

⑯ Interpret several things they say as a come-on. Respond with, "I'm flattered, truly flattered, but I don't think this is appropriate in this situation."

17 If there are two interviewers, act disinterested in anything one of them has to say and enthralled with the other. When the "boring" one speaks, look at the "one you like" and make the jerking-off gesture with your hand.

18 Cheek-kiss hello.

19 Hug goodbye.

20 Catch a glimpse of the interviewer's family photo and make a slightly nauseated face. Without missing a beat, flip the frame down so the picture is not visible and carry on the conversation as if nothing has happened.

21 Let your cell phone ring a few times during the interview. With a ringtone of the song "She's My Cherry Pie." Answer the call; have a heated, profanity-laced argument about what causes grass stains.

㉓ Midway through the interview, as the interviewer begins to speak, softly say "Shhhh", and delicately place your finger on his/her lips. Assure them: "I know."

㉔ Use the phrase "Ya dig?" more than once.

㉕ If asked whether you have any weaknesses, answer "I work too hard, and I'm a perfectionist, so sometimes I can be just a tad impatient." Add "Oh, and I like to rape antelope."

㉖ Act bored and check your watch a lot.

㉗ Look at a picture of the interviewer's wife. Say "She's very pretty." Then stare a little too long, get really serious and repeat "Very pretty."

㉘ On your resume, as prior work experience, list: a) your Warcraft credentials, b) "Freelance Drifter", c) "Captain in Prussian Army (previous life)."

㉙ Look up at the ceiling every once in a while and say, "Did you hear that?"

㉚ At the end of each interview, while shaking hands, continue to hold on to the interviewer's hand while you continue to reopen and force additional conversation. Refuse to let go of the interviewer's hand, maintain serious eye contact, and slightly invade personal space.

㉛ Enter and give the interviewer a headshot. Inhale deeply, and tell them that you'll be performing soliloquy from *Hamlet* or *Prelude to a Kiss*. Perform it. Poorly.

36 Things to Do
on a Driving Test
to Screw with the Examiner

Driving test examiners tend to be a surly sort, judgmentally scribbling away as you nervously heed their every direction. Suffice to say, these power-road-trippers need to be put in their place. You're the one in the driver's seat, after all. And while this test may have a lot riding on it, you can always take it again. So have a little fun the first time around.

1. Straddle the dotted lane-dividing lines on the highway. When the examiner asks what you are doing, explain you are "playing Pac-Man."

2. Demand to play "20 Questions" during the test. Be terrible at it.

3. Signal right when you turn left and vice-versa. As you exit the car, make sure the examiner sees you have your shoes on the wrong feet.

4. Blast gangsta rap.

5. Blast NPR.

6. Blast imaginary space ships.

7. During the parallel parking test, park horribly and ask "Wait, which one is parallel and which is perpendicular again?"

8. Unprompted, ask extremely personal questions about the examiner's life like "Have you ever truly been in love?" and "Do you believe in God?"

9. Drive to the beat of the music.

10. Wear uncomfortably revealing jean shorts.

11. Before the examiner can buckle his seatbelt, pull yours all the way across the middle of the car and insert your seatbelt in his buckle. Make him use your buckle because you heard "the crisscross method was safer."

12. As you stop at a red light, close your eyes, grasp your gold cross and mumble an extremely serious prayer in Spanish before accelerating again.

13 When you are reading for the eye test, squint hard, struggle, and guess letter sequences such as "T...A...I...N...T.." and "L...A...B...I...A..." Incredulously exclaim, "Hey, what kind of test is this?!"

14 Fill your glove compartment with loose olives. Ask the examiner to check in there for your sunglasses. As he does so, see the olives, and say in relief "There those are."

READ THE SIGNS

Here's what road signs now mean to you:

Yield: Honk.

Stop: Stop your car, all motion, speech, and breathing for five seconds.

Crosswalk: Get out and walk.

35 mph: Shirt off.

15 For your ID picture, a) wear a monocle, b) wear two monocles, c) sob heavily, d) make yourself throw up.

16 As you enter the car, take your key out and act puzzled as to where the key goes. Be unable to solve this problem. After a minute, sigh and say in a resigned voice "Just not in the cards today, I guess."

17 Put in a "How to Learn German" CD and engage the exercises, practicing loudly and intensely.

18 As they get in, put on a chauffeur hat and say, "Where to, Gov'na?"

19 Never have more than one eye open at a time.

20 Gulp nervously at anyone you see when you pull up next to a car and hit the car locks in barely hidden panic. (The older and less threatening the person, the better.)

㉑ In the back seat, have massive amounts of: a) porn DVDs, b) dreidels/lubrication bottles, c) toads.

㉒ Ask "Hypothetically, if a dead man was in the trunk, can you use the car pool lane?"

㉓ Use hand signals. (Make sure they aren't even close to the correct ones.) If you have a sunroof, signal through it.

㉔ Congratulate yourself for the simplest of driving tasks like changing lanes, cockily smirking to the instructor: "Not bad, huh?" Wink.

㉕ When you first see the instructor, smile in pleasant surprise and mumble "That's what I'm talking about." Quickly pull out cologne and breath freshener from the glove compartment. Heavily apply both.

26 Annoyingly drone the words of every restaurant and store sign you see: "Best Buy... Home Depot... Bennigans..."

27 Honk often, cuss constantly and give the finger to drivers who aren't doing anything wrong.

28 Excessively recline your seat, "gangsta-style"; advise the instructor to do the same. When he inquires what you're doing, respond, "This is how we roll."

29 Start driving on the wrong side of the road. In an awful British accent, ask how many kilometers per hour you can go.

30 Have two dozen notches cut in your steering wheel along with a pocket knife below the dash. If the examiner asks about the notches, answer without emotion: "Some questions are best left unanswered."

31 Look behind you often and be on the constant lookout for "The Fuzz."

32 Be ashamed of your car and talk about how you're going to get a much better one when you have more "coin in your pocket." Be really insecure about it and refuse to let this go. Keep apologizing.

33 Explain your horn is broken and have a kazoo in your mouth. Use it.

34 Hum the *Spy Hunter* theme the whole time.

35 Do the old "honk your horn" gesture to trucks. Get giddy if the truck drivers comply.

36 Stop at a truck stop. Tell the instructor you'll be right back. Run behind the bushes. After a minute, come back. Have more energy and be happier than you were before.

32 Things to Do to Screw with People in Class
(ESPECIALLY THE TEACHER/PROFESSOR)

They say a student's mind is not a vessel to be filled but rather a flame to be ignited. We couldn't agree more. We believe in fanning those flames into wildfire that, while destructive, cleans the tangled underbrush of University bullshit to allow for true growth. So if a class has mandatory attendance, but that lecture on the symbolism of *Jane Eyre* just isn't doing it for you, here are a few ways to keep yourself entertained.

1. On all papers and tests, have written *fuck!* Tourette's Syndrome *balls!* Write a *shitface!* letter explaining your *ass-puncture!* condition.[1]

2. Preface all of your answers with "Rumor has it" or "Lord knows…"

3. Speak in an awful British accent and use British spellings. Make your "British" spellings increasingly "doubious."

4. Lug a desktop computer to class because "it's all you can afford." Better yet, bring a Commodore 64, Atari 2600, typewriter, or an abacus.

5. If someone sneezes, say "The weak shall be destroyed!" instead of "Bless you."

6. Constantly ask aloud "Is this going to be on the test?"

7. Constantly ask "Can you define that?"

1. If your teacher expresses doubt, bring a note from your doctor. Your doctor should have *fart-it!* the same *cock!* condition.

8 Constantly ask "What would happen if a robot fought a dragon?"

9 Insist you are royalty. Have a friend come in and inform the teacher that one's gaze must never fall upon you, but rather all questions must be addressed to you through your "personal listener."

10 After the professor concludes a point, stand up and give a sarcastic slow clap. Proceed to explain why the teacher's reasoning is wrong. End with a diabolical: "So I am afraid you are quite... mistaken." Cackle maniacally.

11 Address the professor as a) Your Honor, b) My Liege, c) Rabbi.

12 If the teacher asks you a question, parry the question with "Talk to the hand." If he pushes it, escalate to "Talk to the fist 'cause the hand is pissed."

13 Whistle.

14 Whittle.

15 Wobble.

16 For fill-in-the-blank or multiple choice tests, fill your answers in about a half inch off. Wear thick glasses as you hand in your test.

17 If using text books that you will return at the end of the semester, dog-ear pages any time the subjects of death or wounds are mentioned. Highlight and underline those phrases, and write "Yes!" or put check marks by them.

18 Wear a black turtleneck and beret and snap your fingers in beatnik applause as the teacher lectures his "spoken word."

19 Pretend to be a foreign exchange student from a fictional country. Have a translator next to you speaking loud, distracting gibberish.

20 Ask your history teacher if he can make his references "more current."

21 Conspire to have everyone stare 10 feet to the left of where the lecturer is while he's talking.

22 Purposely get caught passing a note around. Have the note just say "I LOVE PORRIDGE" over and over.

23 Conspire with others to start bogus fads that an old teacher might believe: a) pony tails through protractors, b) three-cornered hats, c) a cucumber balanced on the shoulder, d) humming a G-note.

24 Answer questions addressed to you in the form of a question as if on *Jeopardy!*

25 Answer questions dramatically verbalizing your entire thought process as if on *Who Wants To Be a Millionaire?*

26 Answer all questions in the inflection of *$25,000 Pyramid*, saying things like: "Uh boring things, uh... pointless questions, um... things a pompous pedant might say..."

27 After the professor makes a boring point, exclaim, "That's the liquor talking."

28 Enter to theme music and imitate the entrance of a professional wrestler.

29 During boring lectures, echo a spirited "Amen!", "Dat's right" and "Say it, Brother!" as if at a Pentecostal sermon. Get more and more spirited to the point of talking in tongues.

30 Turn your laptop to a neighboring student and initiate a game of Battleship. Call out "E-24" or "You sank my destroyer."

31 Every time the teacher turns around, move your seat up about 4 inches. Gradually do this until you're two feet away from him/her.

32 Prearrange a time to have every student simultaneously a) faint, b) sneeze, c) stand up and do a pelvic thrust.

MINDgames: Biblio-defile

Do teachers read bibliographies and citations? Find out. Score one point for each bogus source you slip in. But don't stop here. Make up your own list of fake resources. The more irrelevant, the better.

"100 Years of Salmon" <u>Field and Stream</u> Sept. 2001: 70-75.

Kreln, Leonard 2006. <u>Cleveland Steamer: The "Underground" Deviance of Harriet Tubman</u>; Easton, MD: 2001

Ghazanvi, Cyrus. "Neo-marxism in Smurf Societies" <u>Canadian Business</u> Mar. 2006: 47-49.

Florn, Jim. "Taint Misbehavin'": An exploration of the "in-between." <u>Plumpers</u> 34-52 May 1984.

Polgen, Ralph. <u>Nooks and Crannies: A Comparative Study.</u> New York Harper 1812.

7 Things to Do on a Paper if You Don't Give a Crap Anymore

1. On papers and assignments, put a silent "b" in every word. Dob tbhis fobr bthe whole pabper.

2. Put quotes around words for no "reason."

3. Every bucket other bucket word, bucket write bucket "bucket."

4. Next to your name, put your Warcraft avatar name and statistics.

5. Intimate a written lisp. Like thith.

6. Subliminal messages. (Read the first letters of entries 2-6 downward.)

7. Tell the teacher you ran out of paper so you had to improvise. Show the text written on your inner thighs.

MINDgames: Slip It In

Score points with your friends for using the following phrases in a paper. Be creative in finding a seamless context. Wager.

"ass backwards" — 10 points

"apeshit" — 20 points

"queer as a three dollar bill" — 7 points

"Koala bear's nuts" — 8 points

"killer croissant" — 3 points

"Our teacher is borderline retarded." — 50 points

Subliminal messages such as the one in the "Things to Do on a Paper List" (pg. 25) — 3 points per letter of message.

23 Things to Do in Airports and on Airplanes

In the post 9-11 world, fooling around in airports is a bad idea. Rightfully so, airports are bastions of formality and seriousness. Nonetheless, here are the most hypothetical of all hypothetical airport high jinks. Do not do these or you will subsequently need a list of "funny things to do in Guantanamo."

1. Happily walk toward the metal detector. Scream in agony and convulse as you pass through it. Shoot a fearful look to the person behind you before hurrying off in a glazed shock.

2. Get in a quick workout by running the opposite way on a moving sidewalk. Wear a headband and spandex.

3. Bring individual grocery items including vegetables, deli meat, and hygiene products, and place them on the x-ray conveyor belt. Have your checkbook and supermarket club card out and ready.

4. Wrap a luggage tag around your wrist and ride the baggage carousel motionless.

5. Buy copies of *Juggs Magazine* and *Newsweek* at the magazine shop. Look around nervously and "secretly" insert *Juggs* into *Newsweek* to read, letting the person next to you see what you're doing.

⑥ Do the same thing, but reverse the magazines.

⑦ Leave the aforementioned magazine combo in the seat pockets of plane.

⑧ Stand a few feet in front of the door to the airport's Admiral's Club and demand the secret handshake. Force some awkward contact with their hand. Nod, "You're good," or "The master will see you now" and let them pass.

⑨ Try to check your luggage: a) one marble, b) a horseshoe crab with a red ribbon around it, c) an 8" by 10" photo of Constantine Chernenko.

⑩ Fill Sudoku grids in the *In Flight* magazine with the number 6 over and over.

⑪ Fill crosswords in the *In Flight* magazine with the word "Flounder" over and over.

12 As you deplane, mistake air traffic controllers with their directional batons as Jedi with Light Sabers. Egg them on with Vadaresque "Yes, feel your anger. Give into the dark side."

3 Things to Do at the Currency Exchange

1. Tell them you need 20 dollars in wampum.

2. Try to exchange a) Monopoly money, b) baseball cards, c) "tales of adventure."

3. Exchange 10 dollars for Euros. Then "change your mind" and exchange the Euros for Yen. Then exchange the Yen for Marks. Continue with a variety of currency exchanges, gladly paying the conversion fee each time until you are left with the equivalent of one dollar in value. Exchange back to one dollar. Say thank you and leave.

13 Contemplate "Tarmac" as a first name for your child.

14 At arrival area, hold up a sign that says "Zarkon, Galactic Time Traveler of the Year 3000." Wear a silver foil vest and matching arm bands.

15 On the plane, read 3rd grade level books and move your lips substantially as you read. After about thirty minutes, realize you were reading upside down.

16 Ask the shoe shine man a) "to finish the job, wink, wink", b) to "take a little off the top", c) to use the polish to give you blackface.

17 Wait at the gate of an arriving plane. Hold a sign with a name on it to draw a crowd. Suggestions: Bill Gates, Mr. T., Socrates. Or have a sign with all three names.

18 Repeatedly page the flight attendant and ask her to have the captain give you a report on meteorological conditions and altitude information, citing that his updates are not frequent enough for your liking.

19 Read something and shake your head saying "No, all wrong. Totally wrong!" Cross things out with a red pen. Reveal you are reading/correcting *Marmaduke*.

20 Approach the ticket counter and attempt to get the first flight to "Ronkozon." Tell the attendant that you were told to get there, and that's all you know. Say you might be pronouncing it wrong, but you don't know what country it's in or how to spell it.

21 At metal detector, along with your keys and coins, put the following in trays: a dozen condoms, Mapquest directions to a church, and anal beads.

㉒ Check a Commodore 64 instead of a laptop through the carry-on X-ray.

㉓ Report suspicious activity of harmless people, telling security things like, "He just ordered a McGriddle, but it was the *way* he ordered it." (We remind you that these are for entertainment purposes only. Don't do that.)

29 Things to Do at a Supermarket

Ever take a close look at supermarket shoppers' faces? They resemble mindless zombies, wheeling around their carts, feasting on the bounty of frozen dinners. No better are the patrons of organic superstores, where brainwashed and delusional yuppies gladly pay 19 dollars for an apple and a green pepper. Undoubtedly, the "market forces" have overwhelmed the masses, and somebody needs to shake up the status quo.

1 Take the checkout dividing bar and place it on the ground between you and the person behind you as opposed to between your respective grocery items. Shoot aggressive looks if the person next in line edges forward.

2 Create bogus free samples tables. Label the table "Free Samples: Clusterjoys!" Suggested combo: apple with corrugated pickle, sprinkled with Lucky Charms and A1 Sauce. Be creative.

3 Have a GPS out on your cart. Consult it and occasionally change direction.

4 While waiting in line to check out, read *Good Housekeeping*, shake your head and huff "Bullshit!" and "Are you fucking kidding me?!" under your breath. Become more emphatic as you read the magazine.

5 Set up a canvas and paint still life of the produce.

6) Be endlessly picky with your fruit selection. Tap on them. Listen to them. Hold them up to the light. Place them in your pants and bounce up and down. Finally, find the ones you want, then repeat the process with the next produce item.

7) Ask Customer Service what aisle you can find a) "the green stuff, y'know, the green stuff!", b) "the thing you eat and like it's round", c) "streln". Get increasingly frustrated.

8) Watch the deli slicer and, with each slice, grunt sounds of arousal.

9) Put a small suitcase, open laptop, and your shoes on the checkout counter. Have your passport out.

10) Hide a hamster in your coat pocket. Put a quarter in a gumball dispenser; then using sleight of hand, pull out the hamster.

11. Ask the butcher for a) emu, b) aardwolf, c) "the most human-tasting meat he has."

12. Sneak huffs of cinnamon in the Spices aisle. Get caught and then race to put the spice back and pretend to browse items overcasually.

13. Put every item in plastic bags with twisty-ties, including all prepackaged ones. Apologize profusely with a foreign accent to the cashier for misunderstanding. When the cashier finally deals with it, pay in pennies.

14. Fill your cart with hundreds of limes. Wheel around the store, examining other things, but always return to put more limes in the cart. Smile to another patron and say "You just can't beat limes."

15. Enter a frozen foods freezer. When someone opens the door, start blinking your eyes and act like you have awakened in the future. Marvel at the ceiling's "magical firelights." Assume you are in the "Sultan's Palace."

MINDgames: Two Supermarket Sports

LLL: Lacrosse with Ladles and Lemons.

Designate two goals on opposite sides of the supermarket (say the sour cream section and the frozen waffle section.) Make teams. Play.

Shopping Cart Demolition Derby.

Each person has a shopping list. The goal is to collect it all and get to a supermarket checkout line. Your opponent can use his cart to crash into yours and vice-versa. If any item in your cart touches the ground (by your cart toppling over) you must replace it with another of its type.

⑯ Bring additional containers of "toppings" and place them by the salad bar: M&M's, a bowl of dice, Monopoly houses and hotels, etc.

⑰ By the flower display, leave a picture of a child with "Dedicated to Lisa Mendez 1997-2008." Add candles.

18 Cool off in the vegetable mist machines.

19 Pull your cart with a leash.

20 With someone seated in it dressed as Chinese royalty.

21 Buy 200 sympathy cards and one belated Bar Mitzvah card. Tell the cashier "You don't even want to know what happened."

22 Sing along to the music.

23 Dance along to the music.

24 Devour melons to the music.

25 Unleash the nuts in a bulk section without a bag. Scream, "Jackpot! I'm a winna!"

COMBO DEALS

Great combinations to pique the cashier's curiosity:

- Astroglide, a rotten squash, and a romance novel
- Butcher knife, hand towel, and Lysol deodorizer
- Home pregnancy test, coat hanger, and baby oil
- Condom boxes, candy, and children's magazines

26 Eat food items in line. Explain you are buying them anyway, so you can start eating.

27 Use items in line like shampoo and shaving cream. Explain you are buying them anyway, so you can start using them.

28 Drop a fake shopping list on the floor that says: "Sacrifice to Dark Lord Shopping List." Include progressively odd items like: candles, butcher's blood, chicken livers, cow skull, elixir of the undead, vorpal sword of doom.

29 Put a baby on the produce scale; make notes.

MINDgames: What doesn't belong?

Arrange four things on the checkout conveyor belt. Tell the cashier that they have to decide which of the four items does not belong. For example, three vegetables and one fruit. They must decide the answer before the items hit the scanner. For every product they get right, they get to keep that product. Make the challenge increasingly difficult.

28 Things to Do
in Church

With its potpourri of scandal, anachronism and pedophilia, the Church's God-cred has taken a hit recently. Nonetheless, we must offer an additional disclaimer for this chapter because the ramifications of these acts go beyond legal. If you're a believer, skip this chapter, or start working on a "Things to do in Hell" list. If you're more religiously reckless, then it's time you did the molesting (uh… mentally, that is.)

1. As people start to solemnly mumble the Lord's Prayer, instead, using the same inflection, recite the lyrics to the 1985 Chicago Bears' "The Super Bowl Shuffle."

2. Replace "Amen's" with "Yeah Boyeeeee!"'s.

3. Heckle.

4. When reading aloud in group, mispronounce words like "Thou", "Jesus" and "God."

5. Two words: beach ball.

6. During a Bible lesson, turn to a neighbor and ask "Where are we, exactly ?" Then hold out your book: *Yes I Can, the Story of Sammy Davis, Jr.*.

7 Sneeze. When some says "Bless you", explain it wasn't you, but rather "Jesus working through you."

7 Great Confessions to Screw with a Priest's Head

1. Impure thoughts about Foghorn Leghorn.
2. Went to JC Penny, pretended to browse, stuffed wallets in pockets for physical pleasure.
3. Feelings of arousal when near pineapple.
4. Excessive palm-licking.
5. Possessed by Major League Baseball umpire. (Demonstrate this.)
6. Used "i" before "e" and it wasn't after "c". Not even close.
7. Picturing priest naked right now.

28 Things to Do in Church

8 Insist your crotch sweat stains resemble the Virgin Mary. Seek corroboration.

9 Ask priest for a double-stuff communion wafer.

10 Weekly church outfit: tight leather pants and a Led Zeppelin sleeveless half-shirt.

11 Replace organ music with the "Footloose" theme.

12 Beat-box during hymns.

13 Use the church collection basket to make change.

14 Ask the person sitting next to you, "Who would win in a fight: Jesus or Zeus?"

15. Quote fake Bible passages (e.g. "You gotta know when to hold them, know when to fold 'em. Frank 3:23.")

16. Pretend to be drunk at the confession booth; tell priest, "I love you, Dude... You're like one of my only real friends... you know? Who needs those fat sluts anyway, right? Bros before ho's... Seriously, I love you like a brother..."

17. **EXTRA BLASPHEMOUS!** Pick-up Mardi Gras beads and yell "Show us your... (realizing) Oh, wait."

18. Claim you are the second-coming of the messiah, then perform second rate magic tricks to prove it.

19. Feel the spirit and talk in tongues, repeating: "Domo Arigato, Mr. Roboto!"

⑳ Wear novelty vampire teeth. Cower and hiss when cross gets near you.

MINDcrafts:

You know those #1 foam hands? Take those, some scissors, some glue, and some Nerf products and fashion them all into some oversized "Foam Praying Hands".

㉑ Purposely sing hymns 4 seconds behind.

㉒ Enter with a huge soda, a tub of popcorn, and 3-D glasses.

㉓ When reading biblical passages, say "Jeepers" instead of Jesus and "Golly" instead of "God."

㉔ Insist your left knee is possessed. Have it do its own thing.

25 Mistake the confession booth as a dunk tank. Act accordingly.

26 Hold your lighter up as if at a rock concert.

27 Take flash photography. Constantly.

28 **EXTRA BLASPHEMOUS!** Shave in holy water.

51 Things to **Do** on an **Elevator**

Riding an elevator with strangers may be the apotheosis (look it up) of awkwardness. We'll do anything to distract ourselves from the possibility of interacting with one another: the unnecessary glances at our watches, our sudden fascination with the illumination of the numbers above the doors, our ability to stare straight into a wall, etc. But there's so much more we could be doing to screw with these poor souls who have locked themselves in our elevating prison. They are so helpless. So vulnerable…

1. Stand an uncomfortably short distance from the only other person in the elevator.

2. In a completely silent moment, turn to the other person, and say "Yes?" Politely accept their explanation that they said nothing. Repeat this 2-3 times.

3. Laugh. A lot.

4. Cry. A lot.

5. Hold a headshot and pretend you are rehearsing for an audition. Repeatedly practice "It's not just tuna. It's tuna-tastic!" Use every conceivable inflection.

6. Sprint into the elevator out of breath. Have a moment of relief, see the other person, become alarmed, and sprint out before the doors close.

7 Stand with your feet further apart than what would be considered a normal stance.

8 Jog in place.

9 Skip in place.

10 Thrust your pelvis repeatedly in place.

11 Constantly wiggle your fingers.

12 Face backwards.

13 Face down.

14 Whistle the chorus to "Funkytown" over and over.

Things to Say When Someone Else Gets On

- "You've found me, Inspector." (Extend your hands as if to be handcuffed.)

- "Well, well, well… We meet again."

- "You've passed the test, Charlie!"

- "I like nougat."

- "Did anyone ever tell you look exactly like Pat Johnson?" When they ask who Pat Johnson is, say "I am."

15 Press "Door Open" whenever the doors are about to shut. Tell other passengers you are expecting a guest. Tell them your guest is Bob McAdoo.

16 Order a Domino's pizza using the emergency telephone.

17 Blindfold yourself and repeatedly shout "Marco!" Flail your arms in an attempt to tag someone.

18 When someone gets on, look out the door nervously and immediately press "Door Close" over and over. Explain to them: "The sentinels are coming."

19 Blow on your hands as if freezing. Shiver.

20 Act like cobwebs are all over you. Grasp at them futilely and attempt to remove them.

21 Smile as people get on, then collapse as if you are suffocating when people press a button. Gasp "Why?" as you fall unconscious.

22 Set up a velvet rope and wear shades. Ask to see ID if they want to get into "The 'Vator: the world's only altitude-shifting night club." Have promotional materials.

MINDgames: Elevator Challenges

Set up a lemonade stand. 2 points for each cup sold.

Sit with an easel and paper and do quick caricatures. 3 points for each caricature sold.

Attempt to convert other passengers to Jehovah's Witnesses. 10 points for each conversion.

23 Have your iPod on. Nod your head like you're really into it, singing (not too loudly) "You're a grand ol' flag… you're a high flying flag…"

24 Hit the buttons as if making a phone call, then pick up the emergency phone and say hello.

25 Slam dance.

26 When anyone presses a button, pretend to shut down as if your power had been turned off. Wait until someone presses another button to turn back on.

27 Yoga.

28 Staring contest.

29 Limericks.

30 Look at the back of your hand. Then the front. Then the back. Then the front. Then the back...

31 Try to scratch the middle of your back. Be unable to reach the itch, growing frustrated. Look at the other person, almost saying something. Then try again.

MINDgames: Elevator Challenges

Challenge friends to an elevator "King of the Ring" and try to force each other out whenever the doors open.

32. Say into recorder: "Idea for story: Two people meet in an elevator. Fall in love at first sight... But then it all goes horribly wrong."

33. Say into recorder: "Idea for story: Wilt Chamberlain-type decides to open a pet shop. He reconsiders his plan and decides against it." Nod proudly.

34. Text on your Blackberry, while speaking your message out loud: "Do not forget turnips... I hate you so much... Do not forget turnips."

35. Introduce yourself as passengers get on. Include your home town and any professional organizations. Network aggressively.

36 Gregorian chants.

37 "USA" chants.

38 "Vindication is mine!" chants.

39 Choose a passenger. Stare intently at his/her a) right eye, b) left knee, c) crotch.

40 Look at a random person, then scribble notes furiously. Repeat sporadically.

41 Enter panting. Ask people if they are "Gerald"; if they know where you can find him. Leave at the next floor, swearing.

42 Wear an orange sash and cargo pants. When others enter, decry, "Where's your uniform?!"

43 Read aloud from *Little Women*.

44 Have one eye closed and look on the floor for something. If they ask if you lost a contact, say no.

45 Start a game of Hacky Sack. Laugh at others' mistakes. Be arrogant.

46 Act like the walls are compacting on you. Use dialogue from *Star Wars*.

47 Look at the ceiling, see if others follow.

48 Translate other people's conversation into Spanish.

49 As a person exits, just as the doors shut, whisper a) "I'm dying", or b) "I love you".

50 Carefully take fingerprints off a button after passenger presses it. Slip fingerprint into envelope marked "Evidence."

51 Encourage others to get off at your floor by saying, "Hurry, the rich men in zeppelins will soon be by!"

MINDgames: Press Your Buttons

Stand in an elevator with your friend. Pick a number that you think the next passenger will press. If you're wrong, take off one article of clothing and if you're right, put one back on. Take turns predicting.

17 Things to Do on an Exam if you Don't Give a Crap Anymore

We've all been there. Taking a test that you have no clue about. Randomly selecting a choice, filling out a Scantron sheet "DC CAB, DC CAB, DC CAB." The essay exam where you say the same sentence in sixteen different ways to fill up that page. The math quiz where you purposely make that digit indecipherable so it could be considered a 4, 9, or 7. Whatever the situation might be, if you're going to fail, fail in style.

1 Highlight all the "the's" and "a's".

2 For simple English tests, employ complex math formulas to arrive at your answers.

3 Drop a smudge of unidentifiable thick liquid on paper. From that point on, write everything backwards.

4 Wrap several slices of roast beef in the test and hand it back to teacher; assure him with a confident, warm smile, "there you go."

5 Color entire test in black crayon with the word "SO MUCH PAIN" written in scissors scratches.

6 Answer every question, "former Surgeon General C. Everett Koop." Have cross-outs occasionally of the correct answer, but ultimately go with "Koop."

7 Take the test fully vocalizing your internal monologue.

8 Eat a sloppy joe while taking the test.

9 Answer question 1 with "see question 6." Answer question 6 with "see question 2." Lead the teacher on a series of "see question's" ending with "by the time you have read this, she will already be dead."

10 On biology test, paste Tom Selleck pics on all diagrams. (Note: this requires you to collect a large amount of Tom Selleck photos if you do not have them yet.)

11 Leave the entire test blank but hand it to the teacher with a pile of change on top. Wink suggestively.

12 Attach "notes of your work": Big Mac wrappers, drawings of sunsets, and poorly written erotic fiction.

13 On exam days, wear your lucky a) tight pants, b) nipple tassels, c) falcon.

14 Take the test in a) crayon, b) finger paint, c) colonial garb.

15 Two words: bagpipe breaks.

16 Take the test, writing on the underside of your desk.

17 As you get a copy of the exam, run out screaming "I've got a golden ticket!"

TRY THIS AT HOME

Get caught looking at "cheat sheets". When the professor confiscates it, he will find a) a picture of Ray Liotta under which is written "Inspiration", b) a collage of photos of Carmine from *Laverne and Shirley*, c) the following message: "*I knew you would suspect my cheating. Well done. However, as you are reading this, my plan has come to fruition. For I am but a distraction for the real cheater in this class, whose cheating method takes precisely the amount of time it takes for a scholarly man to read this letter. It seems that the professor must profess he has been foiled. The first round goes to yours truly. I look forward to our future battles of wit.*" Optional: In the time he reads the note, quickly attach a dapper mustache and bowler hat.

48 Things to Do on a Blind Date

So, you've been set up, and in walks a blind date who vaguely resembles Tommy Lasorda. On a bad day. Or maybe your date's misleading Match.com pic shaved off a few years… and pounds… and cheek hairs. The point is that you want to put this date out of its misery ASAP. Why struggle with forced conversation and feigned interest in his/her account liaison work? There's only one kind of screwing that should happen on this date, and that's a good MindF*ck.

1. Excuse yourself to the bathroom. Come back sopping wet. Offer no explanation.

2. Breathe extremely audibly.

3. Order a plain lime for an appetizer. Put butter on it and calmly consume it, acting as if nothing is unusual.

4. Speak all your statements with an interrogative inflection?

5. Freestyle rap. Lots of it.

6. Always return to one topic of conversation: former Baltimore Oriole Lenn Sakata, as in, "Oh that's interesting about your family, but let me tell you about a man who treated his team like a family, and that's former Baltimore Oriole Lenn Sakata."

7. Greet your date with a horrible version of "Wassssupp!" from the Budwesier commercials. Do it again to busboys and waiters. Need validation from your date.

8. (men) Tag on real sardonic "for a girl" to all your compliments, as in "That skirt looks really nice on you... for a girl."

9. Rub your hands together and smile fiendishly as you talk.

10. Great Off-putting Moves on the Dance Floor:
   - Air trumpet.
   - The Goose Step.
   - Grab your crotch with both hands, keep your knees locked and bend forward over and over.
   - Touch your elbows together and freeze. For fifteen minutes.
   - Violent, angry shadow boxing. Use profanity.

⑪ Eat only the parsley at dinner. Complain about the portion size.

⑫ Make multiple *Dungeons & Dragons* references, as in "That waiter is as lawful neutral as a modron."

⑬ Every time you make a point, say "You follow?"

⑭ When he/she orders, shake head and smirk. If they inquire what the problem is just laugh an intensely sarcastic "No, good choice. Really."

⑮ Make a passing reference to not being the same since "the incident." If asked about it, quickly change the subject.

⑯ Solicit fist bumps.

⑰ Constantly hint that you are an alien as in "Reminds me of Zarkon 9... uh.. I mean St. Louis."

MINDgames: Dating Profile Dares

Include these tidbits on your dating profiles. Wager with your friends.
If you actually score a date with any of the following on your profile
page, each other player pays you five dollars.

- Looking for Rutherford B. Hayes type.

- Inspirational quote: "There are no timeouts in the world of
  professional wrestling."

- Please note: I am allergic to people named Wendell.

- Video of you in the throes of your hobby: scooping cottage cheese
  on tortoises for fun.

- Only picture: a photo of your scabbed knees.

Make up your own. Be creative.

⑱ Nervously scratch your palms.

⑲ Greet your date with gifts: a) a stack of *Popular Mechanics* magazines, b) a framed picture of yourself, c) a monogrammed bowling ball you expect him/her to carry around.

⑳ Wear a Members Only jacket, parachute pants, and a Spuds Mackenzie hat. Make references to '80's culture as if they were topical. e.g. "Have you seen that new *Sixteen Candles* movie?"

㉑ Insist on at least 30 rounds of Rock, Paper, Scissors. At least 30.

㉒ Spit.

㉓ Squint.

㉔ Squat.

㉕ Obsessively wipe everything he/she touches with a towelette.

㉖ Repeatedly use the word "milkweed" as an adjective, as in "This has been really milkweed."

㉗ When excusing yourself to the bathroom, say in your smoothest, most suave voice, "Pardon me, I have to lay cable." (Wink.) When you come back say, "They got the extended package." Act as if you're being incredibly charming.

㉘ Offer to draw a quick portrait of your date. Inexplicably draw a mail box.

㉙ One word: Narcolepsy.

㉚ Ask "You gonna eat that?" in the middle of the meal while he/she is talking.

③① If they ask…
What do you like to do?
You say, a) "lint sculpture", b) "I like to stand on parking lot cement logs and try to catch blowing plastic bags mostly", or c) "build boats in bottles and vice-versa."

③② At completely inappropriate times, say "That's really funny" or "I'm so sorry."

③③ Give her fake, but believable information like: a) Matt Lauer has an extra finger, b) Patrick Swayze designed this restaurant, or c) Earth is the only planet named after a Jew.

③④ When reviewing the check, take out an abacus; calculate with deadpan concentration.

③⑤ Fill pockets with Russian dressing. As your date eyes you confused, explain "For Renaldo."

36 "Raise the roof" a lot.

37 In an accusing tone, constantly compare your date unfavorably to Simon Bolivar, as in "Simon Bolivar didn't smoke."

38 If he/she leaves for the bathroom, switch a) tables, b) clothes, c) hair-style, d) personality, e) gender.

39 Attempt to do napkin origami. Fail. Be ruthlessly hard on yourself with "I suck!"s and "I'm such a loser!"s.

40 Order a) a fudge and ham sandwich, b) gin and ground beef, c) a jar of mayonnaise with cherries in it.

41 Add a "and the same for the lady/gentleman" when ordering.

42 Stare two inches to the left of your date's eyes when conversing.

43 For a good night kiss, kiss your palm. Then lightly slap his/her face.

44 In the middle of a pleasant conversation, tell him/her to "turn it down a notch."

45 Ask for a party of three; explain to your date that your imaginary friend "Keldin" will be joining you. Work Keldin into the conversation. Be creative.

46 Have a picture of someone clearly older than you in your wallet. Say it's your kid from a previous marriage.

47 One by one, throughout the night, reveal the restraining orders you have on your six exes.

48 Tell cute stories about your dog "Rommel."

41 Things to Do
at the Office to Screw with
Coworkers' Heads

Whether you're just starting up at some temp gig, or you've been eternally stuck in a dead-end job, cubicle walls can begin to feel like prison bars. From 9 to 5 you're forced to follow the paradigm, find synergistic solutions, and optimize workflow. It's ridiculous, and yet we all adhere to this life/death sentence. It's time to loosen up the noose-tie and strap on a Bolo. There are ways to get through the work day.

1. Conclude your phone conversations with "I wish you good tidings."

2. Because of your "neck condition", place your flat screen monitor in your lap and look at it as you type. Continue to rearrange your monitor and keyboard positioning in progressively absurd ways to help with your ailments and injuries.

3. Daily lunch: 4 plums and a teaspoon of flour.

4. Leave unsigned bogus phone message memos on people's desks such as "Call Kirk about the shrimp problem. ASAP!"

5. Beneath or in place of your job title on your email signature, add: a) 8th Level Cleric, Forbidden Realms, b) Certified Muff Diver, c) Vice-President, Rocking It Out.

6. Add a roof to your cubicle.

7 Wear swim goggles.

8 For an hour straight, stare into your screen, typing intently.
   Eventually, let someone see you have been typing "Salmon" over
   and over.

9 Fill your Outlook planner with fake activities and let others see.
   Example: "10:00- Imagine canoeing with Greg Gumbel."

10 Stare into the water cooler. As soon as someone sees you, quickly walk
   away, as if trying to hide something. Repeat hourly.

11 Use "typing gloves."

12 Email a real news article to coworkers and claim it is from the *Onion*
   and that "It's hilarious."

13 Reply to all emails in iambic pentameter.

MINDgames: Meeting Madness

Compete with your friends to earn points. During the next office meeting, try to subtly interject the following phrases into the meeting. Everyone must hear the words and you must be speaking to the group.

"Shoot our load too early" – 5 points

"Shoot way too much of our load" – 10 points

"Unleash our load all over..." – 20 points

"Apeshit" – 5 points

"Chinaman" – 10 points

"Wet fart" – 7 points

"A sea bass's chance in Doodoosville" – 10 points

(14) Computer desktop wallpaper: dozens of pictures of dead birds.

(15) Actual physical desk top: collage of dozens of pictures of dead birds pasted on the desk.

(16) Fill your desk drawers with absurd combinations of things: a wrench, a condom, bundles of dandelions, a hypodermic needle, etc. Leave the drawers open.

(17) Write all memos in piglatin.

IM THE MAN

Pretend to be IM'ing and talk aloud as you type: "Yeah, the party was fun.... 8 Penguins... Beat the shit out of them... Yes, insertion came first... Will tell you more later... working now... just a couple of ass-munch coworkers..."

18 CC all your business emails to "Our lord and savior who sees all."

19 CC all memos to "Pat Sajak, our lord and savior who sees all."

That's Prangsta!

When your coworker leaves his desk, create a bizarre Out of Office Email Message. Here's a sample:

"I will be out of the office from December13-17, questing for the Sword of Eternal Light in the Caves of Rendor. If you have immediate questions, consult Selkon the Elf in the Clearing of Darkwood. I wish you good tidings."

20 Have "family photos" on your desk featuring framed pictures of the cast of *The Love Boat* and *The Partridge Family*.

21 Leave folders on your virtual (or physical) desktop with odd titles like "Sacrifice to the Overlord"; "Kevin Bacon Fan Mail"; "Xeroxes of My Rash".

22. Add inspirational quotes at the end of your emails. Have them become more and more Scientologist-oriented each day.

23. Forward *Family Circus* cartoons and cat humor emails. Tell your coworkers you thought "They'd get a kick out of this." Average 14-15 of these forwards a day.

5 Great Secret Santa Gifts

1. Framed picture of yourself

2. A bag of charcoal

3. The number 4

4. Head of lettuce

5. Framed picture of a head of lettuce

24 Fill the water cooler with Tang.

25 Stick your key in your computer's USB drive. Futilely attempt to start up your computer.

26 Always mumble about how much you hate Pegasus. Don't elaborate if pressed; just hint, "It's in the past."

27 After being given an assignment, say "Is this because I'm Black / White / Asian / Orc / Half-Orc?" (Choose one that you are not).

28 Dress inappropriately for the season. During your break, read old newspapers from the season you are dressed for.

29 Set up a bar of bourbon and tumblers like professionals did in the 1920's.

③⓪ Hint that you have an obscure religion. Then for "your holiday", create fake traditions like sprinkling your chair with croutons to celebrate the harvest.

③① On group emails, slip in some non-existent addresses. Generally people will not notice them until someone replies to all. Example: Millard@profoundbulge.com

③② "Accidentally" email photos of yourself dressed as Tennessee Williams to your boss. Apologize profusely and explain they were meant for someone else.

③③ Laugh hysterically every day at 9:43 AM.

MINDcrafts:

Cubicle badminton. Take badminton racquets and saw off the handles so they are short. Play badminton over the cubicle wall.

34 Rate people's voicemail messages by holding up scores like a gymnastics judge.

35 Create an "I Love Cabbage" screen saver.

36 Name all of your office equipment.

37 Name all of your office equipment "Larry."

38 Constantly try to use touch-screen on non-touch-screen monitors. Eat Cheetos before doing so.

39 When they say, "Would you like to go to lunch?" You answer: "No thanks. I no longer consume food orally."

40 Brown-bag your coffee like it's a 40 oz..

41 Fill up the office refrigerator with hundreds of jars of mustard. Number them. Offer no explanation.

MINDgames: Office Challenges

Everyone puts 5 bucks into the pot. The winner is the one who completes the most challenges.

- Run one lap around the office at top speed.

- Moan like Chewbacca when you defecate in the office bathroom stall. At least one other person who is not playing must be in the bathroom at the time.

- Ignore the first eight people who speak to you on a given day.

- Make 50 photocopies of your face without someone asking you what you're doing.

- Call everyone you interact with (in person or on the phone) "Daddio" for the entire day.

- Complete all your paperwork for the day in green crayon.

10 Things to Do in an Office Staff Meeting

① Pronounce "business", "bidness."

② Offer your support of ideas with fervent "Huzzah's".

③ During a Power Point presentation, insert pictures of Tyne Daly into the slide show. When they come up, act shocked and defensive. Repeat at all future meetings.

④ During a large meeting, wait for someone to address you in any way. When they do, respond shocked, "You mean you can see me?" Run out and never return.

⑤ Offer high-fives.

6. Offer low-fives.

7. Offer fives of average height.

8. Respond twenty seconds late to everything you experience.

9. Lean back in your chair precariously. Barely catch yourself from falling every 30 seconds or so.

10. Have tons of papers stacked messily in front of you. Shuffle them and constantly be trying to find the right paper. Every two minutes, thrust your hand into the air and gasp, "I'm totally lost." The more irrelevant the papers in front of you, the better.

61 Things to Do in Stores

Advertisers and marketing gurus are paid millions to brainwash the masses to mindlessly browse and buy. Let this be a call to action: Shoppers of the world unite! It's time to wake up and smell the overpriced coffee. Here are some things you can do to screw with people in all sorts of retail establishments.

7 Things to Do In Starbucks

1. Order fake drinks that sound like Starbucks offerings. Bonus points for as many '80s references you can slip in: "Decaf Danza Macchio"; "Vente Mocha Milano"; "Grande Maria Conchita Alonzo."

2. Wear used tea bags as earrings.

3. Ask for a Grande coffee, but in a Tall cup. Watch the confusion slowly set in as the barista makes the drink.

4. Mispronounce orders. Be way off: *lady* for latte, *ca-PUCH-a-no* for cappuccino, *moo-fine* for muffin, etc.

5. Get a friend and sit down. Pretend to be talking with your friend in sign language (just sign randomly). Escalate into a gigantic nonverbal battle. Get more and more emphatic. End with the finger and storm out. (Or end with making out passionately.)

6 Make an absurdly long request: "a double decaf skim, Grande latte with a splash of caramel syrup, no whip, shaken, not stirred, rebuked, and then served in a stack of 3 cups, no cup sleeve, light on vanilla, a dash of nutmeg, and then punch me in the stomach."

7 Have an audible conversation about how great pipe cleaners are. Speak about this for 15 minutes.

9 Things to Do at a Book Store

1 Set up a book-signing table with a bunch of copies of a book and act as if you are the author. Write strange notes in customers' book copies like "Note to self: Don't forget eggs!"; "Join the forces of Darkness"; or "I am attracted to both your parents."

2 Fake like you're speed-reading a thick philosophy book at an absurdly fast rate. Nod occasionally.

③ Do the same except pretend that you can comprehend the words simply by sniffing them.

④ Do the same but pretend you can understand by rubbing the book on your crotch.

⑤ Ask Information where you can find a book on a) fondling garden gnomes, b) poetry about marbles, c) "people."

⑥ Build a fort made of books.

⑦ Sit at the café and read a book, chuckling often. Reveal the book to be a dictionary.

⑧ Offer complementary bookmarks: strips of raw bacon.

⑨ Put a clump of pubic hairs on page 157 of Jane Austen's *Emma*. Encourage others to do this across the world until it is the norm.

7 Things to Do at PetSmart

1. Teach parrots to say, "I defecate on your mustache."

2. Walk around with a leashed muskrat.

3. Pretend to be blind and have a hyperactive terrier as your seeing eye dog. Bump into things.

4. Climb on cat jungle gyms.

5. Play with cat toys.

6. Comb your hair with pet grooming devices.

7. Go into the pet adoption center with a cook book. Refer to it as you eye your choice.

6 Things to Do at a Barber Shop/Salon

1. As they apply shampoo, make ambiguous, possibly self-stimulating, movements under your barber smock.

2. While waiting, "sneak" a handful of hair from the ground and smell it. Smile and put it in your pocket.

3. Tell the barber to a) "take a little off the stomach", b) "make me look like Bobby Brady", c) collect the hair from the floor and connect it to yours.

4. Sing.

5. Point to the jars with the blue liquid and gasp, "You're from the future!"

6. Wear a hat. Ask them to "work around it."

2 Things to Do at Foot Locker

1. Ask the referee/salesman for a recommendation, then yell at him in disagreement as if he's made a terrible call in a sports game.

2. Scream in horror at the sight of that foot-measuring device. Explain you had a bad experience. Leave the store, choking back tears.

11 Things to Do in Department Stores

1. Ask to try different lipsticks and other make-up. Look very seriously in the mirror as you apply them. Then reveal you've used lipstick as eye shadow and vice-versa.

2. Try to initiate an '80s movie style fashion montage with a stranger. Keep shaking your head, giving the thumbs down gesture, and making funny facial expressions when they emerge with new outfits.

3. Incorrectly try on clothes such as using a belt as a head band and putting shoes on your hands. Stare at the mirrors scrutinizing the fit.

4. Wear a cowboy hat, get a toy gun, and bust out of the saloon style fitting room doors.

5. Be insanely bad at refolding clothes. Struggle for ten minutes.

6. Pillow fight.

7. Purse fight.

8. Mannequin fight.

9. When department store employees spray you with a perfume/cologne sample, scream "I'm melting.... I'm melting... So much pain... Death is welcome..."; crumple to ground.

10. Nap on a mattress.

11. Try on clothes in kids' sizes. Ask others if they make you look fat.

12 Things to Do at Best Buy

1. On computers, type ridiculous messages like "Asner is Thy Lord" or "The terrorists have taken over the store. It is up to you now."

2. Wear a blue collared shirt and khaki pants (the uniform of employees.) Stand around stocking things and/or hold a clipboard. When people ask for help, explain you do not work there.

3. Stock the refrigerators.

4. Stock the refrigerators with a cooler marked "Human organs."

5. Pretend to sample music on an iPod. Bob your head, rock out, and sing the words to "The Ballad of the Green Berets."

6 Watch the TVs, making loud comments to others about the shows.

7 Ask Customer Service if a) the Commodore Vic 20 is in, b) they have Pong, c) they can help with your relationship problems.

8 Ask an employee to model for you to test out a digital camera. Holler at them as if they were modeling in a photo shoot, telling them to a) be a tiger, b) make love to the camera, c) make anal love to the camera.

9 Rest your head on a tripod.

10 Act as if you are in pain each time something is scanned at checkout.

11 In your best jock voice, shout "Nerd!" at the geek squad. Knock down their books.

12 If they ask, 'Do you need help?"
You say… "The doctors think so." (Lick palms.)

MINDcrafts:

Idea for a high-concept movie. Set the film in Best Buy. Bring your own Mini DV tape, but then film the entire thing when "testing out" store cameras.

7 Things to Do at Wal-Mart

1 Buy absurd combinations of things that arouses cashier's imagination. Examples:
   - a calculator, some glue, and a jar of pickles
   - a hamster, a fork, and some paprika
   - pack of thumbtacks, a menorah, and a bottle of vodka
   - a plunger, some Vaseline, and a poster of a unicorn

2. When the security guy checks your receipt, hand him a second piece of paper with your phone number on it. Wink.

3. Try to buy things that are clearly not for sale like a fire extinguisher.

4. Set up an office at a desk and work.

5. Buy luggage, fill it with items, and have your driver's license out as you pay.

6. Ride an exercise bike. Put a box down asking for pledges to charity.

7. (Eccentric billionaires only) Buy 100,000 protractors. Do not explain why.

Do You Think You'd Be Arrested in Wal-Mart if...

- You lit all of their scented candles?

- You took pictures of your scrotum and left them on digital cameras in the store?

- You placed mannequins in erotic positions?

- You put hundreds of pictures of Harlem Globetrotters in all the picture frames?

- You made coffee in a coffee maker?

- You "anti-shoplifted" lots of items?

Polluting the Amazon

Don't restrict yourself to brick and mortar stores. A good virtual MindF*ck is just as gratifying. Amazon reviews are a great place to let your imagination go to work. Below are just a few "helpful" reviews that we've posted on Amazon over the years.

The Great Gatsby by F. Scott Fitzgerald
  I lost fifty pounds reading this book!

Reviewer: Justin Heimberg from Brussels   March 7, 2000

I've tried every diet in the book(s.) But Mr. Fitzgerald has hit upon the perfect balance of low-carb dining and exercise. His insights into plums are unparalleled. Thank you, Fitzy! You truly are a "great" gatsby.

—This text refers to the Paperback edition.

Beowulf
Beowulf Misleading

Reviewer: Justin Heimberg from Lombardi, NY   March 10, 2000

From the title, I expected a story about Scott Baio and/or Scott Wolf, or some kind of hybrid thereof. No dice. If you are looking for a book about that, then you're better off reading *Cold Mountain*.

Snow Falling on Cedars
My mind was on something else

Reviewer: Justin Heimberg from Cape Cod

A chowder interesting chowder read. Chowder lyrical chowder at chowder times chowder, moving chowder in chowder its chowder simplicity chowder in chowder others chowder. Overall, chowder, well-written chowder with chowder an chowder interesting chowder story, but chowder not chowder knock chowder your chowder socks chowder off. Chowder.

Write your own reviews. Send the links to mindf∗cks@wouldyourather.com.

41 Things to Do to Get Rid of an Unwanted Boyfriend or Girlfriend

We've all been there: stuck in a bad relationship just because we don't want to endure the painful moment of initiating a break-up. Then there's the inevitable aftershocks: the craziness that erupts post-break-up. The only way to beat that kind of crazy is to trump it with your own crazier crazy. You can avoid having to do the dirty work yourself. Just add a quirk or two to your personality, and they'll be the ones who have to do the dumping.

1. In the heat of passion, accidentally scream out a) the wrong name, b) your own name, c) "Wolf Blitzer."

2. Get a large back tattoo of Tony Danza's face.

3. Demand he/she do the same.

4. Three words: wet hacking cough.

5. Use the word "butt-ball" in front of your in-laws. Use it often and as various parts of speech.

6. Insist on romantic ground beef baths.

7. Put on 60 pounds.

8. Take off 60 pounds.

9 Alter the placement of 60 pounds.

10 Constant off-key serenades of "Whoomp! There It Is".

11 Slowly reveal your fantasies of mutual masturbation to rainforest documentaries.

12 Tell her/him that he/she's not dating you but rather "Jesus through you."

13 Keep getting him/her confused with former Milwaukee Buck Jack Sikma, as in "Were you the one I saw a movie with last night or the solid rebounder with a surprising soft touch?"

14 Start to leave out lots of a) empty gin bottles, b) empty absinthe bottles, c) full urine bottles.

15 Leave out a fake love letter from a) another woman, b) another man, c) a Jawa.

16 Become inexplicably irate at the sight of toast.

17 After sex, tell her about your case of a) crabs, b) warts, c) Pubic Elves.

18 New music kick? Full-volume depressing Irish dirges.

19 Tell him/her you're quitting your job to become the next Weird Al Yankovic. Spend hours perfecting the lyrics to "Girls Just Want to Have Bundt" and "Drew an Eclipse on a Chart."

20 Leave your computer on with open web pages about "furries".

21 Conduct play-by-play commentary during sex.

22 Anniversary gift: one of those big foam hands that says "You're #1."

23 Already be wearing a condom prior to disrobing.

24 Utter all sexual exclamations in Yiddish.

25 Insist on new homemade birth control: an English muffin with several strands of scotch tape radiating from the center.

26 Regularly omit the "rinse" portion of the "lather, rinse, repeat" shampoo sequence.

27 Leave the toothpaste cap off (and covered with blood).

28 Leave the toilet seat up (and covered with blood).

29 Say you want to get into something a little more comfortable. Leave the room, come back dressed as a) a pilgrim, b) The Hamburglar, c) Mark Gastineau.

30 During oral sex, mutter under your breath, "Uh oh... that can't be good."

31 Explain that you cannot perform sexually unless witnessed by Tim Russert. Unveil a giant picture over your bed.

32 Insist on mood music: "9 to 5" looped over and over.

33 Insist on mood lighting: bright spotlights.

34 Insist on mood video recording: Barry Gordy's *The Last Dragon*.

35 Give up utensils for "religious reasons."

36 Before sex, calmly hand her/him goggles and bag of warm spinach. Say matter-of-factly: "All right, let's get started."

37 Explain your peculiar erogenous zones: a) elbows and knees, b) eyeballs, c) the jar of loose change on your dresser.

38 Yodel.

39 Add sensual foods to increase carnal pleasure: hard-boiled eggs, bagel and gefilte fish, and cheeseburgers.

40 Hum "Little Drummer Boy" during sex, gradually get louder as the activity becomes more intense.

41 After sex, remove a condom and ask where she keeps the recycling bin.

A
Would You Rather...?
Interlude

Okay, time for a breather. All this MindF✲cking can wear you out. And since this a *Would You Rather...?* book, we thought we'd provide a break in the form of old-school deranged dilemmas. For those of you who haven't read the books, the rules are pretty simple. Read a question to a friend and debate the alternatives.

Would you rather have sex with...

Charlize Theron *OR* Lucy Liu?

Mandy Moore *OR* Jaime Pressly?

an unenthusiastic Ashlee Simpson *OR* a down-and-dirty Nancy Pelosi?

Natalie Portman *OR* Jennifer Lopez if they had each other's butts?

classy Christina Aguilera *OR* slutty Christina Aguilera?

YOU MUST CHOOSE!

Would you rather...

have to masturbate wearing a condom

OR

have to masturbate to sex symbols pre-1940?

Would you rather...

marry the spouse of your dreams but gain 10 pounds a year

OR

have them gain 10 pounds a year?

YOU MUST CHOOSE!

Would you rather have sex with...

Leonardo Dicaprio *OR* Russell Crowe?

old James Bond (Sean Connery in his prime) *OR* new James Bond (Daniel Craig)?

a soft and tender Tony Danza *OR* a fast and furious Mr. Belvedere?

George Clooney *OR* John Goodman if they exchanged weights?

Dick Cheney *OR* the Burger King Mascot?

YOU MUST CHOOSE!

Would you rather...

have your echo in the voice of *Law & Order*'s Sam Waterson

OR

your shadow be on a ten second delay?

YOU MUST CHOOSE!

Would you rather...

sneeze out of your ass

OR

fart out of your nose?

Would you rather...

have a self-refilling coffee mug that keeps your sugar/cream ratio perfect

OR

have throwing star business cards?

YOU MUST CHOOSE!

Would you rather...

have permanent Milwaukee's Best aftertaste

OR

have an odd palsy where you always walk as if you're laying down a bunt?

Would you rather...

have the Sportscenter guys do a full report (complete with highlights) on ESPN whenever you return from a date

OR

whenever you have a bowel movement?

YOU MUST CHOOSE!

123

Would you rather...

have to solve a moderate-level Sudoku before unwrapping a condom

OR

only be able to maintain an erection (men)/reach orgasm (women) by singing the *Family Ties* theme song over and over?

YOU MUST CHOOSE!

What's Your Price?

Would you... put 1,000 staples into your body anywhere you like for $45,000? How about only 50 staples placed wherever a heartless torturer chooses?
Things to consider: Would you then remove them?

Would you... give your 4 year old daughter Double D breast implants for $1,000,000? C cups? B-cups? HHH cups for $50,000,000?
Things to consider: "Hey, she'll grow into them."

Would you... wearing a mask, punch your grandmother as hard as you can in the stomach once for $10,000 if she never found out it was you? Would you do it for $100,000? $1,000,000?

WHAT'S YOUR PRICE...?

Would you rather...

have mayonnaise tears

OR

Koolaid sweat?

Would you rather...

sleep a night on a bed of peanut butter

OR

next to a humidifier full of urine?

YOU MUST CHOOSE!

Would you rather...

be compelled to enter every room by jumping into the doorway with an imaginary pistol drawn like the star of a 70's cop show

OR

invariably make your orgasm face instead of smiling when being photographed?

Would you rather...

have fingernails that grow at a rate of one inch per minute

OR

have pubic hair that grows at the same rate?

YOU MUST CHOOSE!

Would you rather...

have mood lips (change color according to your mood)

OR

make the sound of the shaking of Boggle letter cubes when laughing?

Would you rather...

have to have sex in the same position every night

OR

have to have sex in a different position every night (you can never repeat)?

YOU MUST CHOOSE!

Would you rather...

snore the sound of a dial up modem

OR

cough the sound of a machine gun?

Would you rather...

have your genitalia located on the top of your head

OR

the bottom of your left foot?

Things to consider: jogging, hats, the sexual act, masturbation

YOU MUST CHOOSE!

What's Your Price?

Would you... make out with your sibling for two minutes for $5,000? One minute? 30 seconds? What would be your lowest dollar-per-second rate?

Which of the following names would you change your name to and go by for $125,000?

Scrotal McGee?

Johnny Ballcluster?

Milkbags Maximus?

Extrava Gantlabia?

The "Formerly Known as Prince" symbol?

The sound of a handful of change hitting the table?

What is the weirdest name you'd change it to for $125,000?

WHAT'S YOUR PRICE...?

Would you rather...

draw your dating pool from people browsing the Self Help section of the book store

OR

the Sci-Fi section?

Would you rather...

see (insert attractive acquaintance) naked

OR

see (someone you hate) wounded?

YOU MUST CHOOSE!

Would you rather...

vomit dice

OR

excrete Monopoly real estate?

Would you rather...

be able to hear every cell phone ring in your neighborhood

OR

smell every fart?

YOU MUST CHOOSE!

Would you rather...

have sex in front of your grandparents

OR

the *American Idol* judges?

Would you rather...

relax in a Jacuzzi of a stranger's saliva

OR

have diarrhea in a gravity free chamber?

YOU MUST CHOOSE!

27 Things to Do Before You Die

There are books out there boasting about the places you need to see before you die: the wonders of the world and all the great sites that Nature and History have to offer. BORRRING! And then there are those saccharine books about all the life-affirming things you need to do before death or 40 or whichever comes first. What sort of legacy do you want to leave behind: Tourist? Cliché? No, if you really want to make your mark and seize life by the short ones, then you need to do so in a way that celebrates the absurdity of existence.

X WTF

X

1. Go to a fashion show; shout out bids as if the models are being auctioned.

2. Enter a spelling bee; spell every word B-O-B-A-F-E-T-T.

3. Drop wet lettuce on a roulette table. Ask the dealer to crisp it for you.

4. Grate cheese using an escalator.

5. Ask strippers if they can make change for your dollar.

6. Write self-effacing letters to *Penthouse Forum* mentioning your "twenty second bumblings" and your "two inches of pathetic boyhood."

7. Go to the zoo and talk to chimps as if you're visiting a loved one in prison.

136

MINDgames: Name that Feces

Have one person lead two others blindfolded to a zoo exhibit. Smell the feces in the air and try to say what the animal is.

8 Go to McDonalds. Try to get pickle slices to stick on the ceiling in patterns of constellations.

9 Set up a Scrabble game in Washington Square Park by those chess guys. Talk shit: "What's up? Gotta trade in a 'q'? He's all dressed up but nowhere to go. 'Cause I got the u's." Or "Who wants a 100 tile whoop-ass?"

10 Leave funny names at restaurants if there's a wait. Ideas: Fartation Jones, DeLarry, or The Vindicator.

11. Call Pizza Hut from a payphone right outside the store and ask them to deliver a pizza.

12. Impossibly misuse chopsticks at a Chinese restaurant.

13. Attend therapy: Intimate a) an attraction to Yosemite Sam, b) your phobia of people named Roger, c) loss of all sexual inhibition in Whole Foods.

14. Go to Hollywood. Pitch a buddy cop comedy about a hard-nosed L.A. cop partnered with a a) wily cockatoo, b) bloated penguin, c) retarded robot, and/or d) a sexually compulsive kangaroo.

15. At sporting events, attempt to start nonsensical chants like "We want pie! We want pie!"

16. Take a test drive at a used car dealership. Fill the car with grass. Return the car and politely say you're not interested because of the grass materialization issue.

⑰ Act like you're digging for sand crabs at the beach, then pull out a kitten.

⑱ Integrate bogus French phrases into dialogue.

⑲ At your doctor's office, substitute stool samples with Cookies and Cream ice cream.

⑳ Go on *Jeopardy!*. Phrase answers in unconventional question forms: "Is it..."; "Would it happen to be..."; "Do you suppose maybe it is..."; "What in the Sam Hell is...."

㉑ Go to a Drive-Thru at Taco Bell. Ask for information regarding the whereabouts of "the General."

㉒ Do a crazy dance at a baseball game to get on the Jumbotron. Then pretend to pass out.

5 Fashion Statements

1. The continent beard.

2. Yo-yo necklaces.

3. Socks on the outside of your shoes.

4. Pubic dreads.

5. Live tree frog earrings.

23. Run a marathon width-wise.

24. When kids trick or treat at your house, stage an intervention on the doorstep, insisting that the children's insatiable desire for candy is "a disease."

25 At a fine restaurant, attempt to pay the bill with your AAA card. When they return it to you, smile "My mistake", and put your library card in the bill folder. Continue to do this with everything in your wallet, culminating with a picture of Skippy from *Family Ties*.

26 In a movie theater, at the first joke, turn to a stranger next to you and say insecurely "Did you think that's funny?" After that, say nothing more, but constantly look at the person next to you at a funny part to see if they think a joke is funny.

27 Pick up day laborers so you can drive in the carpool lane.

27 Things to Do Before You Die

8 Things to Do at Museums

1. Convince onlookers that a Jackson Pollock painting is actually 3-D Magic Eye Art, and that if they stare long enough, an image will appear.

2. Scratch and sniff paintings featuring food.

3. Bring your own sketch of a tree to the Met. Put it on the floor, then tell the guard "I think this fell down."

4. At a modern art museum, admire the coat rack or museum map with knowing nods. See if others follow.

5. Put $9.99 price tags on Picassos.

(6) Lead a fake tour, completely fabricating ideas. e.g. "Warhol painted this self-portrait for his lover, Bob Cousy"; "The ibex is found only in Detroit, survives on a diet of scrambled eggs and matzo ball soup, and makes a strange mating call that sounds like 'Yahtzee.'"

(7) At a wax museum, resculpt Princess Diana's face so that she looks like Kurt Rambis.

(8) Change positions of stuffed animal nature displays to more "indecent situations."

34 Things to Do at The Gym

In today's ultra-serious society, the gym holds a unique place.
Nowhere else do people take themselves so seriously and yet look
so stupid. There's that quivering intense work-out face, ridiculous
yoga stretches, homoerotic motivational spotting—all of this
punctuated with a chorus of grunts and unintentional farting.
It's a place where people take themselves way too seriously, and
consequently, it's a good idea to add MindF*cking into your work-
out routine.

1. Offer to spot strangers bench-pressing. Encourage lifters to "let Jesus lift through them."

2. Hard-boil eggs in the Jacuzzi.

3. Work out in a) a tuxedo, b) a Spiderman costume, c) a fit of despair.

4. Sing too loudly with your iPod.

5. Sing too loudly without your iPod.

6. Have preposterously dirty pits on your T-shirt (use maple syrup.)

7. Have preposterously bloody pits on your T-shirt (use ketchup.)

8. Narrate your attempts like a cartoon superhero: "Must... lift weight... over...head..."

1. "You look so vulnerable right now."

2. "Nothing to prove here. No need to be a hero."

3. "Why do we drive in parkways and park in driveways?"

4. "Inhale way up, exhale way down."

5. "Do you play D&D? I have a weekly get-together and we're looking for a mage."

6. "Do you think Heidegger's *Being and Time* is derivative of Kierkegaard's *Truth and Subjectivity*?"

7. (Singing) "That's What Friends Are For." (Look into their eyes.)

9 Crack walnuts in nautilus machines.

10 Lay slabs of beef on sauna rocks.

11 Eye a barbell menacingly. Strike yourself in the chest, crank your neck, and exhale forcefully to psyche yourself up. Do this for 40 straight minutes and then walk away.

12 Work out music: "Ride of the Valkyries", full volume.

13 Melon-eating music: "Let's Hear it for the Boy", full volume.

14 Mistake Coke-machine as exercise equipment. Attempt to use the machine in every conceivable way. Exasperated, finally tell others it is out of order.

15 When asked to show your membership card, show a Mark Eaton rookie card (1979).

16 Demonstrate your new "exercise": arms outstretched, palms out, rigid lock-kneed high kicks.

17 As you work out, splash vanilla extract under your arms and on your towel and on the machines you used. Claim you exude that fragrance.

18 Wear Floatties in the hot tub.

19 Tell ghost stories in the steam room.

20 Swim with knee pads.

21 Double up on a treadmill.

22 If they ask... "Need a spot?"
You answer, a) "I could use one at the urinal.", b) "I don't do drugs.", c) "No thanks. Earnest Borgnine will be here soon."

㉓ Put up a picture of Ralph Macchio on the wall. Do sit-ups, lightly touching your lips to the picture as you crest your sit-up.

㉔ Constantly explain to huge muscle dudes that they're "doing it all wrong."

㉕ Work out muscles on only one side of your body until you are massively asymmetrical.

㉖ Run in place.

㉗ Gallop in place.

㉘ Do the robot in place.

㉙ Smile eerily wide and joyously during workout.

30. Return ludicrous items to the Lost and Found: a sack of barley, a *Silver Spoons* lunch box, a spork, etc.

31. Tell your trainer you want to look more like Mario Van Peebles and less like Mario Albularach.

32. Wear tight spandex shorts and insert any of the following objects into the crotch: a) a hammer, b) a Barbie doll, c) banana bunch. Wink at the ladies.

33. Ask people if they know a good forehead exercise.

34. Tell employee your clothes were stolen; describe exactly what they're wearing.

Quickies

Sometimes you don't have time for a prolonged period of MindF*cking. Sometimes you only have time for a MindQ*ickie. The following short lists will arm you with just a few things to do in various situations and occasions you're likely to encounter during your life.

4 Things to Do at a Hotel

1. Replace hotel soaps and shampoos with those from another hotel.

2. Leave a used mint on hotel pillow with a note "Please leave some for next guest."

3. Supplement the room's décor with Ricky Martin posters. Check out.

4. Buy "Do not Disturb" style door-knob signs at novelty stores like "Stay out! Stereo Blasting", "Hazardous Area: Teenager's Room" etc. Hang them on various doors.

8 Things to Do When Playing Sports

1 Wear far more pads on your body than is reasonable.

2 Do the above when swimming.

3 Have visible skidmarks when wearing tennis whites.

4 Have your golfing caddy wheel you around in a rickshaw.

5 Talk trash in Shakespeare-speak when playing pick-up basketball.

6 Enter the right-hander batting box. Turn to bat left-handed. Explain to the ump that your dyslexic.

7 Half-bury yourself in a golf course sandtrap garbed in a confederate army uniform.

8 Try to quickly bury the ball when playing soccer.[1]

1. Note to self: Idea for sport: Buryball.

11 Things to Do in a Public Restroom

1. Crouch under a hand-dryer and use it to style your hair with a brush.

2. If only one person is using a urinal on a wall with many urinals, choose to use the urinal next to them.

3. At urinals, start conversations with strangers. Be a little too friendly.

4. Stand slightly too far away from the urinal.

5. Stand way too far away from the urinal.

6. Sing spirituals while urinating.

7. And defecating.

8. In the stall, groan, pause, and say "How bout that?" Leave a Rubik's Snake floating in the toilet bowl.

PUBLIC SERVICE ANNOUNCEMENT

How bad are people at urinating? In airport bathrooms, you walk up to a urinal and it's like a two foot radius of yellow swamp. It's not that hard to do. You just need to sort of use gravity. How exactly are people missing so badly? Your shoelaces get all soaked with pee like a mop. It's disgusting. Make the effort to not urinate unbelievably inaccurately. And that's one to grow on.

9 Write odd graffiti on the wall like, "I love scones!" or "For a talented elf-mage, call 555-9199."

10 As you exit stall, comment, "Darn, I got it on my hands." Display your hands covered in glitter.

11 Fill the soap dispensers with bourbon.

Quickies

6 Things to Do at a High School Reunion

1. Thank random people for taking your virginity and apologize for "turning into such a psychopath."

2. Bring a Barbara Bush look-alike as your date.

3. Fabricate a fake career like a) professional sifter, b) head of one of those dragons at Chinese parades, c) Postmaster General's sexual sherpa.

4. Reminisce about completely bogus fads, conspire with others. Fads include: asparagus around the neck, the silver shin craze, the boy group "The Felt Marvels."

5. Apologize to random people for kicking their ass in high school.

6. Arrive early. As people show up, tell them that everyone else in your class is dead.

10 Things to Do to Screw with Telemarketers

1. Inquire about what they're wearing. Proceed to ask about their "openness to new ideas."

2. Speak in an indecipherable Scottish accent.

3. Mistakenly think they are your friend, Norman. Continue talking to Norman about personal matters for minutes. Ask about his rash.

4. If they ask... Do you live alone?
   You answer, "Do voices count?"

5. Laugh at everything they say. Sometimes into applause.

6. Unprompted, tell them what you are wearing. Proceed to misconstrue the conversation as phone sex.

7 Ask if they can call you on your landline. Give them a phone sex number.

8 Answer their questions but add subtly, "Resistance is futile."

9 Tell them you can't talk cause there's a a) breast in your mouth, b) shoehorn in your ass, c) hobbit in your closet.

10 Claim you are in the middle of fixing your lawnmower. Provide pathetic man-made sound effects.

5 Things to Say into Your Cell Phone

Here's something you can do anywhere in public any time. Whip out your cell phone and fake a conversation. Here are some example of things to be shouting into your phone.

1. "OK, so then we'll go with the broccoli and the execution by lethal injection."

2. "I thought it was an oral thermometer, yeah…"

3. "Ponce De Leon?! Are kidding me?! Fuck you!'

4. (Deadpan) "Pudding. Pudding. Pudding. Pudding. Pudding…"

5 "Gorgoth, hey. Listen we are journeying out to the Caves of Rendor looking for the Ring of Light. ... I have a Vorpal Sword... Elven. Anyway, so I have a mage, cleric, and fighter, but I need a good rogue. (Angry) What am I supposed to do without a rogue! (Profanity.)... Well, we will be traversing through the Forest or Kakloon, and there are Drow Elves and Owlbears. Well, I have a chain mail armor and a ring of protection but (laughing) I'm counting on a few Cure Light Wounds spells."(More laughter)

Do your own and be creative. Send your films to wouldyourather.com.

4 Things to Do at a Wedding

1. Set up army men scaling the wedding cake.

2. When the official asks if there are any objections, stand up and go into a ten minute diatribe about Vin Diesel's unwarranted movie career success. Swear often.

3. Instead of confetti, throw a) marbles, b) poppers, c) minnows.

4. Swap the audio of the traditional "Here Comes the Bride" with a) "Wipeout", b) *The Dukes of Hazzard* theme, c) Whale mating calls.

5 Things to Do at a Funeral

1. Wear an oversized football jersey.

2. Motivate the pall-bearers in the style of a personal trainer.

3. Give a bogus eulogy citing fake anecdotes like the time he played for the Washington Generals and his three-way with James Garner.

4. Keep telling everyone your going "to miss Morton." Unless, the deceased's name is actually Morton, in which case, say you will miss "Neldar."

5. Discuss with mourners how the deceased would be perfect for *Weekend at Bernie's 3*.

3 Things to Do at a Birthday Party

1. Bring inappropriate gifts that send a message a) diet books, b) Rogaine, c) self-help literature.

2. Fill the piñata with mussels.

3. After striking the piñata, continue to beat it into a papier-mâché pulp. Refuse to stop. Take it too far.

4 Things to Do on the Road

1. Place a bunch of live crabs in the toll booth change basket.

2. Get in the background of the *Today Show* weather segment with a sign that says "Willard is the father of my child."

3. At a traffic light, wait until a car drives up next to you. When someone looks over at you, suddenly pull the seat lever and plummet backwards.

4. Let a leash dangle from your car.

3 Things to Do If You can Travel Through Time

1. Sew up Napoleon's front pocket.

2. Tell Genghis Kahn to "take it down a notch."

3. Go to the signing of Declaration of Independence, sign "Lou Ferrigno" before John Hancock has a chance to sign, thereby, forever creating the expression, "I need your 'Lou Ferrigno' on this document."

45 Things to Do to Screw with a New Roommate

Maybe you're going to college. Maybe you're just trying to save money by hitting up Craigslist to find an apartment to share. Maybe your parents kicked you out of their basement for watching porn and leaving Sun Chips crumbs on the sofa. Whatever the reason, moving in with the wrong roommate can be a disaster. Or an opportunity. If the new roomy rubs you the wrong way, or you just want to screw with him/her for the hell of it, the possibilities are endless.

1. Feign masturbation to: a) biology text book diagrams, b) a photo of your roommate's family, c) a biography of Susan B Anthony.

2. Put Parmesan cheese in your coffee.

3. Only read the Obituaries section of the paper.

4. When brushing your teeth, brush your face as well. (Also good: use a hairbrush for a toothbrush and/or vice-versa.)

5. Choose seats on the sofa that are too close to your roommate.

6. Use kitchen cabinets for your clothes and your dresser for utensils.

7. Offer to cook dinner for your roommate. Spend three hours in the kitchen. Finally serve him/her four lemon slices with peanut butter on them.

8 Plaster your walls and ceiling with posters of Alex Trebek.

9 Cover your desks with books about George Washington Carver. Leave all sorts of messy failed peanut experiments all over the place.

10 Blend all your meals before consuming them.

11 Two words: Spiderman Underoos.

12 Laugh at the completely wrong times when watching movies and TV.

13 Cry at the completely wrong times when watching movies and TV.

14 Scratch yourself vehemently at the completely wrong times when watching movies and TV.

15 Respond at entirely inappropriate times with "Is that a threat or an invitation?" or "Do the math."

16 Sleep under your bed.

17 Sleep under your roommate's bed.

18 Sleep in a wheelbarrow of saw dust.

19 Compulsively count things like carpet threads, window panes, and your roommate's hair. Be unable to stop.

20 Fill your humidifier with bourbon and inhale the fumes, getting drunk.

21 Talk to the toaster.

22 When your roommate comes home, always be reaching under the sofa for something. Quickly stop when he sees you and act overly nonchalant.

23 Sleep-walk.

24 Sleep-talk.

25 Sleep-shadow-box.

26 When talking to your roommate, move your eyes back and forth as if watching a ping pong game.

27 Pray loudly before eating, entering, exiting, and making a bowel movement.

28 Watch your roommate and take notes. Insist what you're writing is unrelated to him. When he does anything, resume writing.

29 Watch TV marathons of *Full House*; recite from memory all of the Olson Twin's lines in a spooky monotone.

30 In your roommate's presence, listen to only one song over and over: "Party All the Time" by Eddie Murphy.

31 Day or night, every time your roommate comes in, immediately turn off the lights and go to bed.

32 Always return the subject of any conversation back to windmills.

33 Never be seen not eating a meatball sub.

34 In your roommate's presence, eat only one meal: Apple Jacks and mustard.

35 Sort your dresser drawers by color, not article of clothing.

36 Insist corn chips and various snacks miraculously resemble religious figures. Collect them.

37 Sit on a head of lettuce. Explain your doctor told you it will help with your posture.

38 Erotically moan the names of various former Postmaster Generals in your sleep. Every once in a while slip in a little spice: "Yeah, lick that stamp baby", "Route that mail, route it all night long."

39 Leave your bedroom door ajar and sit in a corner by yourself and roll D&D dice, giggling.

40 Seemingly be unable to distinguish between a stapler and your keys. Attempt to perform tasks requiring the tools, pretending to try to hide your embarrassment.

41 Stack your bookshelf with 20 identical copies of *The Ancient Art of War*.

42 Tell your roommate that "Leonard" dropped by for him/her. Give the message several times a day.

43 Use your roommate's deodorant. As a popsicle.

44 Limit your all articles of clothing to the color fuchsia.

45 Call your roommate a) "Bro", b) "Dogg", c) "Darling", d) "Schnookies."

About The Authors

Justin Heimberg is a comedy writer who has written for all media including movies, TV, books, and magazines. He, along with David Gomberg, runs Falls Media, an entertainment company specializing in providing short and funny creative services and products.

David Gomberg is notably different from other oozes. Being a growth, he is fixed to one place and cannot move or attack. For the most part, he is forced to feed off of vegetable, organic or metallic substances in an underground wall. If he grows on a ceiling, however, he can sense if someone passes below, and drops onto them. Living creatures touched by Gomberg eventually turn into Gomberg themselves. Gomberg is vulnerable to light, heat, frost, and cure disease spells. Gomberg is mindless and cannot speak. As such, he is regarded as neutral in alignment. Gomberg will re-grow if even the tiniest residue remains, and can germinate to form a full sized ooze again years later.

About *Would You Rather...?* Books:

Us guys, the authors of the *Would You Rather...?* books, believe that the great joys in life are the times spent hanging out with your friends, laughing. Our books aim to facilitate that. They are Socially Interactive Humor Books. SIHB's. Damnit, that acronym sucks! Let's try again... Socially Interactive Games & Humor SIGH... exactly the opposite of what we are looking for in an abbreviation. Son of a bitch. Alright look, these books make you think in interesting ways and talk to your friends, and laugh and be funny. They are, and they make you, imaginative and irreverent. Lots of bang for your buck (and vice versa.) *WYR* books provide 3-300 hours of entertainment depending on how painfully retarded your reading pace is. So take these books, hang out with your friends, and have a good time.

Other *Would You Rather...?*® Books:

Would You Rather...?: Love & Sex asks you to ponder such questions as:

- **Would you rather...** orgasm once every ten years OR once every ten seconds?

- **Would you rather...** have to have sex in the same position every night OR have to have sex in a different position every night (you can never repeat)?

- **Would you rather...** have breast implants made of Nerf® OR Play-Doh®?

Would You Rather...?: Love & Sex can be read alone or played together as a game. Laugh-out-loud funny, uniquely imaginative, and deceptively thought-provoking, *Would You Rather...?: Love & Sex* is simultaneously the authors' most mature and immature work yet!

Would You Rather...? 2: Electric Boogaloo
Another collection of over three hundred absurd alternatives and demented dilemmas. Filled with wacky wit, irreverent humor and twisted pop-culture references.

Would You Rather...?: Pop Culture Edition
A brand new collection of deranged dilemmas and preposterous predicaments, featuring celebrities and trends from popular culture. Ponder and debate questions like: *Would you rather... be machine-gunned to death with Lite-Brite pegs or be assassinated by Cabbage Patch Dolls?*

Would You Rather...?: Illustrated — Tired of having to visualize these dilemmas yourself? No need anymore with this book of masterfully illustrated ***Would You Rather...?*** dilemmas. Now you can see what it looks like to be attacked by hundreds of Pilsbury Doughboys, get hole-punched to death, sweat cheese, or have pubic hair that grows an inch every second. A feast for the eyes and imagination, ***Would You Rather...?: Illustrated*** gives Salvador Dali a run for his money.

Would You Rather...?'s What Would You Be?
Stretch your metaphor muscles along with your imagination as you answer and discuss thought/humor-provoking questions like: If you were a Smurf, which one would you be? What if you were a type of dog? A road sign? A Beatle? A nonsense sound?

sevenfooterpress.com
falls-media.com
classlesseducation.com

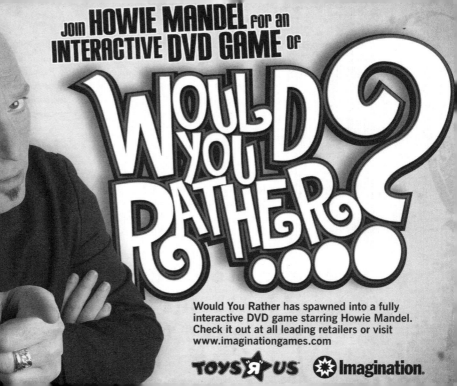